Book 1
CompTIA A+
By Solis Tech

&

Book 2
Human-Computer Interaction
By Solis Tech

Book 1
CompTIA A+
By Solis Tech

All-in-One Certification Exam Guide for Beginners!

Table Of Contents

Introduction

I want to thank you and congratulate you for purchasing the book, *"CompTIA A+: All-in-One Certification Exam Guide for Beginners!"*

This book contains proven steps and strategies on how to prepare for the CompTIA A+ exams.

This eBook will explain the basics of the CompTIA A+ certification and tests. It will also give you some pointers regarding the topics that you need to review. By reading this book, you will gain the knowledge and skills required to pass the tests.

Thanks again for purchasing this book, I hope you enjoy it!

Chapter 1: The CompTIA A+ Examination

This eBook is written for people who are knowledgeable about computers. It assumes that you know to how to use a computer and its peripherals (e.g. printers, modems, etc.). This book will serve as your guide in preparing for the CompTIA A+ exam.

The A+ Certification

This is a certification program developed by CompTIA (Computer Technology Industry Association). This program is designed to provide a consistent way of checking the competency of computer technicians. The A+ certificate is given to people who have reached the degree of knowledge and diagnostic skills required to give proper support in the PC industry.

The A+ certification is similar to other programs in the industry (e.g. Microsoft Certified Systems Engineer and Novell's Certified Novel Engineer). The principle behind these certification programs is that if you need to get services for their products, you want to find technicians who have been certified by these programs.

The Benefits of Being A+ Certified

There are many reasons to get your own A+ certification. The information packet distributed by CompTIA gives the following benefits:

- It serves as a proof of your professional achievement.

- It improves your marketability.

- It gives you excellent advancement opportunities.

- It is now considered as a requirement for other kinds of advanced computer training.

- It encourages customers to do business with you

How to Become Certified

The A+ certification is given to anyone who passes the exams. You are not required to work for any company. CompTIA is not a secret group or society. It is, on the other hand, a group of elite computer technicians. If you want to be A+ certified, you have to do these things:

- Pass the exam called A+ Essentials

- Pass one of the three technician examinations:

- o IT Technician Test

- o Depot Technician Test

- o Remote Support Technician Test

You can take the tests at any Pearson VUE or Thompson Prometric testing center. If you will pass both exams, you will receive a mail from CompTIA. That letter will inform you that you passed the tests. Additionally, it contains the certificate, a lapel pin, and a business card.

How to Sign Up for the Exams

To sign up for the tests, you may call Pearson VUE at 1-877-551-7587 or register online at www.vue.com. For Thompson Prometric, call 1-800-777-4276 or visit the website www.2test.com.

These companies will ask for your name, employer, phone number, mailing address, and SSN (Social Security Number). If you don't want to give out your SSN, a provisional number will be given to you. Additionally, they will ask when and where you want to take the exam.

Obviously, the exams aren't free. You have to pay your chosen testing company. That means you have to specify the payment arrangement during the registration process. You can simply provide your credit card information to the customer representative you will talk to. If you're doing it online, you can enter the credit card info on their payment page.

Who Should Use This Book?

If you want to pass the A+ tests, and do it confidently, you should use this book as a guide for your preparations. The A+ Essentials test is created to measure basic skills for an entry-level computer technician. The technician tests are designed to certify that you have the required skills to service microcomputer hardware.

This eBook was created with one purpose in mind: to help you pass the A+ exams. This guide will do that by explaining the things on which you will be tested.

Chapter 2: The Different Parts of a Computer

A PC (i.e. personal computer) is a machine made up of different components that work together to perform tasks (e.g. helping you write a document or add up large numbers). With this definition, notice that computers are described as having various distinct parts that work together harmoniously. Nowadays, almost all computers are modular. That is, they possess parts that can be replaced if the owner wants to improve the performance of his device. Each part has a specific purpose. In this chapter, you'll learn about the parts that make up a common PC, how they work, and what their functions are.

Important Note: Unless stated otherwise, the terms "computer" and "PC" can be used interchangeably throughout this eBook.

The Different Parts of a Motherboard

The motherboard, also called the system or planar board, serves as the "spine" of a PC. This is the brown or green circuit board that you'll find at the bottom of your computer. The system board is the most important part of a PC since it houses and/or connects the other parts of a computer together.

Different Types of Motherboards

There are two main types of motherboards. These are:

Integrated Motherboards – With this type, most of the parts are integrated into the system board's circuitry. Basically, integrated motherboards are created for simplicity. Since majority of the components are already part of the board itself, you won't have to install them individually. However, this simplicity has a major drawback: once a component stops working, you cannot simply replace it; you have to replace the entire motherboard. These boards are cheap to manufacture but expensive to repair.

Note: If one of the parts breaks, you may just disable it and add an expansion card that has similar capabilities.

Nonintegrated Motherboards – Here, the major parts (e.g. disk controllers, video circuitry, etc.) are installed as expansion cards. You will easily identify this kind of system board since every expansion slot is occupied by a major component.

The Different Form Factors of Motherboards

Computer experts also classify motherboards according to their design (also known as *form factor*). Here are the main form factors being used today: NLX, BTX, ATX, and micro ATX. You have to be vigilant when buying a computer case and system board separately. Some cases lack flexibility: they might not accommodate the system board you will select.

Let's discuss each form factor:

1. NLX – This is the abbreviation for "New Low-profile Extended". In general, this form factor is used for cases that are low-profile. With this design, the expansion slots (e.g. PCI, ISA, etc.) are placed on a special card to reduce the vertical space they occupy. Daughter boards, or adapter cards, that are normally plugged vertically into the expansion slots, are placed parallel to the system board. That means their size won't affect that of the computer case.

2. BTX – This form factor was launched by Intel back in 2003. With this design, the head-producing parts are lined up against the power supply's exhaust fan and the air intake vents. Then, the other components are cooled by installing heat sinks on the motherboard. This design offers a quiet setup since it involves efficient airflow paths and fewer exhaust fans.

3. ATX – With ATX motherboards, the processor and memory slots form a 90° angle with the expansion cards. This design places the memory and processor in line with the power supply's exhaust fan. Thus, the processor can remain cool while it runs. In addition, you may add expansion cards (even the full-length ones) to an ATX motherboard since the memory and processor are not parallel to the expansion cards.

4. Micro ATX – This form factor is similar with the previous one, with one major difference: it is designed for smaller computer cases. Micro ATX motherboards benefit from the enhanced cooling designs of their full-sized counterparts. However, since they are smaller, they have lesser motherboard headers, integrated components, expansion slots, and memory modules.

Processors – Their Functions and Characteristics

Now that you are familiar with system boards, you have to learn about their most important part: the central processing unit (CPU). The CPU controls all of the computer's activities using both internal and external buses. Basically, it is a processor chip that contains millions of transistors.

Important Note: Nowadays, the word "chip" describes the whole package that a computer technician may install into a socket. However, this word was originally used to refer to the silicon wafer hidden inside the carrier (i.e. the "chip" you see on your motherboard). The pins that you see on the outer part of the carrier are connected to the silicon wafer's small contacts. These pins allow you to install the carrier into a socket.

You can identify which part inside the PC is the central processing unit: the CPU is a large square that lies flat on the motherboard with a large fan and heat sink.

The Features of Modern Processors

- Hyperthreading – This word refers to HTT (hyper-threading technology). Basically, HTT is a variant of SMT (simultaneous multithreading). This kind of technology uses the scalar architecture of modern CPUs.

  HTT-capable CPUs appear as two different processors to the computer's operating system (OS). Because of this, the OS may assign two processes simultaneously, such as symmetric multi-processing, where multiple processors utilize the same network resources. Actually, the OS should support SMP in order to use HTT. If a process fails because of missing information caused by, for instance, branch prediction problems, the processor's execution resources can be reassigned for a different procedure that can be conducted immediately. Thus, the processor's downtime is dramatically reduced.

- Multicore – A CPU that has a multicore design contains two processors inside the same package. Here, the OS may treat the CPU as if it were two different CPUs. Just like the HTT, the OS should support SMP. Additionally, SMP is not considered as an upgrade if the apps run on the SMP system are not meant for parallel processes. A good example for the multicore technology is the i7 Quad-Core Processor from Intel.

- Microcode – This is the group of instructions (also called instruction set) that compose the different microprograms that the CPU executes as it performs its functions. The MMX (multimedia extensions) is a special example of an individual microprogram that performs a specific instruction set. Basically, microcodes are at a lower level than the codes used in computer programs. On average, each instruction from a computer program requires a large number of microinstructions. Intel and other processor manufacturers incorporate the MMX instruction set into their products.

- Overclocking – This feature allows you to increase the performance of your CPU, on par with processors created to function at overclocked rates. However, unlike processors created to function on that speed, you have to make sure that the overclocked processor doesn't damage itself from the increased level of heat. You might need to install an advanced cooling system (e.g. liquid cooling) to protect the CPU and other computer parts.

- Throttling – Processor throttling, also called clamping, is the process that specifies the CPU time to be spent on a computer program. By specifying how individual programs use the processor, you can "treat" all of the applications fairly. The principle of Application Fairness turns into a major problem for servers, where each program may represent the work of another user. That means fairness to computer programs becomes fairness to the users (i.e. the actual customers). Customers of modern terminal servers take advantage of this feature.

Memory – Its Functions and Characteristics

Nowadays, memory is one of the easy, popular, and inexpensive methods to enhance a computer. While the computer's processor runs, it stores data in the machine's memory. Basically, the more memory a machine has, the faster it can operate.

To determine the memory of a computer, search for thin sets of small circuit boards that are packed together near the CPU. These circuit boards sit vertically on the computer's motherboard.

How to Check for Errors in a Computer's Memory

Parity Checking

This is a basic scheme used to check for errors. It lines up the computer chips in a single column and separates them into equal bit groups. These bits are numbered beginning at zero. All of the number x bits, one from every chip, create a numerical array. If you are using "even parity", for instance, you will count up the number of bits contained in the array. If the total number is even, you will set the parity bit to zero since the bit count is already even. If the total is an odd number, on the other hand, you should set the parity bit to 1 in order to even up the bit count.

This technique is effective in identifying the existence of errors in the arrays of bits. However, it cannot indicate the location of the errors and how to solve them. Keep in mind that this isn't error correction – it is just a simple error check.

ECC

ECC stands for *Error Checking and Correcting*. If the computer's memory supports this method, the system will generate and store check bits. Whenever the machine accesses its memory, an algorithm will be performed on the check bits. If the result turns out to be zero (or a group of zeros), the information contained in the memory is considered valid and the computer functions as normal. ECC can identify single-bit and double-bit errors. However, it can only correct errors that are single-bit in nature.

The Four Main Types of Memory

- DRAM – This is perhaps the most popular type of RAM out there. DRAM stands for *Dynamic Random Access Memory*. Because of their inherent simplicity, these memory chips are cheap and easy to create compared to the other types. This kind of memory is called dynamic since it needs constant update signals in order to keep storing the data written there. If the DRAM chips won't receive stable signals, the information they hold will be deleted.

- SRAM – This stands for *Static Random Access Memory*. Unlike DRAMs, this kind of memory doesn't require a steady stream of signals. In general, SRAM chips are more complex and expensive than DRAMs. You can use SRAM for cache functions.

- ROM – This is the abbreviation for Read-Only Memory. It is called as such because it prevents the user from editing the memory it contains. Once the data is written on the computer's ROM, it cannot be changed anymore. ROM is usually used to hold the machine's BIOS, since this data is rarely modified.

- CMOS – This is a special type of memory chip. It is designed to hold the configuration settings of a computer's BIOS. CMOS is battery-powered: that means the configuration is retained even if the machine is turned off.

Storage Devices – Their Functions and Characteristics

Computers are useless if they can't store anything. Storage devices hold the information being used, as well as the programs and files the computer needs in order to function properly. In general, storage devices are classified according to their capacity, access time, and physical attributes.

HDD Systems

HDD stands for *Hard Disk Drive*. This storage device is also called hard disk or hard drive. Computers use HDDs to allow quick access to data as well as permanent storage. Typically, hard disks are found inside a computer.

An HDD system is composed of:

Controller – This component controls the storage. It knows how the drive functions, emits signals to the different motors inside the disk, and accepts signals from the sensors within the drive. Nowadays, hard disk manufacturers place the drive and controller in one enclosure.

Hard Disk – This acts as the physical warehouse for the data. HDD systems store data on little disks (about 3-5 inches in diameter) grouped together and kept inside an enclosure.

Host Adapter – This is the system's translator: it converts signals from the controller and hard disk to signals the computer can work with. Most modern motherboards have a built-in host adapter, allowing drive cable connection through board headers.

Floppy Drives

Floppy disks are magnetic storage devices that use plastic diskettes enclosed in a tough casing. Several years ago, floppy disks were used to easily transfer information from one computer to another. Nowadays, few people are using floppy disks because of their small capacity. DVD-ROMs and CD-ROMs have replaced floppy disks in storing and transferring digital information.

CD-ROM Drives

Modern computers use CD-ROM drives. These compact disks are virtually similar to those used in music recording. CD-ROMs allow you to store data for a long period of time. In general, these drives are read-only: you cannot erase or delete the data once it is stored on a CD. In addition, computers need to spend a longer time in "reading" CDs compared to internal hard drives. Why are these drives so popular?

Despite their drawbacks, CD-ROMs are used because they can store large files (about 650MB) and are extremely portable.

DVD-ROM Drives

This is the newest storage device to be used for computers. The DVD (i.e. digital video disc) technology is mostly used for entertainment purposes (e.g. home theater systems). DVD-ROMs are basically similar to the DVDs you use at home. Because of this, computers that are equipped with a DVD-ROM drive can play movies stored on a DVD.

However, DVD-ROMs are way much more useful when used for computers. Since they use newer technology, DVD-ROMs are better than CD-ROMs in terms of storage capacity. On average, DVDs can hold 4GB of data. That means DVD-ROMs are your best option if you are storing or distributing large files.

Important Note: CD-ROMs and DVD-ROMs have the same appearance. The single difference is the logo on the front of DVD drives.

Removable Storage Devices

Many years ago, the term "removable storage" meant something extremely different from what it means now. Tape backup is one of the old storage devices that can still be bought today. Modern computer users prefer the solid-state, random-access removable storage devices. In this section, you'll learn about tape backups and the new storage solutions.

Tape Backup

This is an old type of removable storage. A tape backup device can be installed externally or internally and utilize either an analog or digital magnetic tape to store data. In general, this kind of device can hold more information than other storage mediums. However, they are also one of the slowest in terms of data transfer rate. Because of these reasons, tape backup devices are mainly used for archived information.

Flash Memory

Before, random-access memory chips were only used to access and use data. But now, you'll find them in different physical sizes and storage capacities. Flash memory drives are considered as the best solid-state storage device available. The flash memory category includes SD (secure digital) and other memory cards, USB flash drives, and older detachable and non-detachable memory mechanisms. Each of these storage devices has the capability to store huge amounts of information.

Manufacturers of flash memory devices use revolutionary packaging (e.g. keychain attachments) for their products to provide easy transport options for their end-users.

Chapter 3: How to Work With Computer Parts Effectively

While taking the CompTIA A+ exam, you will answer questions regarding the installation, usage, and replacement of computer parts. This chapter will help you to review regarding those topics.

How to Install, Configure and Optimize Computer Parts

Aside from knowing the characteristics and functions of PC components, you also need to know how to use them. In particular, you should be familiar with the installation, configuration, and optimization of such parts.

How to Upgrade a Storage Device

Storage devices are available in different shapes and sizes. Aside from IDE and SCSI, two of the most popular types, there are SATA (Serial ATA) and PATA (Parallel ATA). You can also   differentiate between external and internal drives. This section of the book will explain each of these options.

Preparing the Drive

Regardless of the technology being used, you should format storage devices before using them. Although most drives have their own formatting software, each OS has a tool that you can use. When working with Windows computers, you can utilize the format utility through the command line. If you are working with XP, Vista, 7, or newer Windows system, you can also use the graphical utility program called Disk Management.

How to Work with IDE

Before, IDE (integrated drive electronics) drives were the most popular kind of computer hard drives. Although they are often linked to hard drives, IDE is more than just an interface for hard disks. It can also serve as the interface for different storage types such as Zip, DVD, and CD-ROM.

To install IDE drives, you should:

1. Set the slave/master jumper on the IDE drive.

2. Place the drive inside the drive bay.

3. Connect the cable for power-supply.

4. Link the ribbon cable to the motherboard and to the drive.

5. If the drive isn't detected automatically, you should configure it using the BIOS Setup of your computer.

6. Use your PC's operating system to format and partition the IDE drive.

How to Work with SCSI

SCSI is the abbreviation for *Small Computer System Interface*. This kind of device can be either external or internal to the machine. To configure an SCSI device, you should assign an SCSI ID (also called SCSI address) to all of the devices in the SCSI bus. You can configure their numbers using a jumper or DIP switch.

Whenever the computer sends data to the SCSI device, it emits a signal on the cable assigned to that number. The device will respond with a signal that holds the device's number and the information needed.

You should install a terminator (i.e. terminating resistor device) at the two ends of the bus to keep the SCSI devices working. You can activate and/or deactivate terminators using a jumper.

Here are the things you should do when installing an SCSI device:

- For Internal Devices – Connect the cable (i.e. a 50-wire ribbon cable with multiple keyed connectors) to the adapter and to each SCSI device in your computer. Afterward, place the terminators on the adapter and terminate the final device in the chain. You should leave other devices unterminated.

- For External Devices - Follow the steps outlined above, but here, you should use some stub cables between the SCSI devices in the daisy chain (instead of a long cable that has multiple connectors). Terminate the adapter as well as the final device in the daisy chain (that device should have one stub cable linked to it).

- For Hybrid Devices – Many types of adapters have connectors for external and internal SCSI devices. If you have this kind of adapter, attach the ribbon cable to your internal devices and connect the cable to your adapter. Afterward, daisy-chain the external devices from the external port. Terminate the device at the end of every chain. Make sure that the adapter is unterminated.

External Storage Devices

As capacities shoot up and prices fall down, the number of available external storage devices has increased greatly. Aside from the SCSI variant explained above, you will also see devices with USB connections and those that can connect straight to the system. The computer's operating system will recognize USB devices upon connection. You can just install any additional programs you like to use. A computer program called Dantz Retrospect is included in many storage devices to allow you to utilize external devices as automatic backups.

If the external storage device is linked straight to the system, you can just follow the instructions that came with that product. Then, install additional programs on the computers that you will be using. The main benefit of linking straight to the system is that the storage device/s can be accessed by all of the computers.

How to Upgrade Display Devices

Before linking or unlinking a display device (e.g. a computer monitor), make sure that the computer and the device itself are powered off. Afterward, connect a cable from the computer's video card to the display device. Connect the power cord of that device to an electrical outlet. You may use a modern Digital Visual Interface (DVI) cable or the traditional DB-15 (or VGA) cable.

While installing a new monitor, you should have the proper driver. The driver is the software interface between the display device and the computer's OS. If you don't have the right driver, your monitor won't display what you want to see. Nowadays, you can download the newest drivers from the website of monitor manufacturers.

Aside from the power supply, the most dangerous part to repair is the monitor. Computer technicians say that beginners should never attempt to repair monitors. Monitors can hold high-voltage charges even if they have been powered off for several hours. That means you can be electrocuted if you will try to repair a monitor by yourself. If your monitor stopped working, and you don't want to buy a new one, you should take that device to a TV repair shop or a certified computer technician. The technicians and the repair guys know how to fix monitors properly – they understand the dangers and the correct procedures.

How to upgrade Input and Multimedia Devices

The typical upgrade for input devices is the transition to newer mice and keyboards.

Keyboards

Keyboards may wear out if used repeatedly. The usual problem is "key sticking", where keys are no longer responding to the user. To replace a PS/2 101-key keyboard with a new one, just unplug the old keyboard and plug in the new. As you can see, this is a quick and easy process. Nowadays, however, computer users prefer to replace old keyboards with USB ones.

Here is a principle you need to remember: You can use the "unplug-the-old-and-plug-in-the-new" procedure as long as your computer's OS supports the keyboard you want to use.

Mice

17

Computer mice also wear out because of repeated use. But don't worry: you can replace old mice with new ones. You may easily replace a PS/2 connection mouse with another without spending too much. As an alternative, you may buy an optical mouse (which prevents dust- and ball-related problems) or a wireless one (which needs batteries to send and receive signals). Although new mouse models still use the PS/2 type of connection, most mouse products in the market use the USB connection.

Chapter 4: The Tools Needed for Checking Computer Parts

The CompTIA A+ exam will also test your skills in checking computer parts. This chapter will help you with that topic by discussing the tools and diagnostic procedures needed.

The Tools Needed by a Computer Technician

A great computer technician needs a great collection of tools. If you are working alone, you may not get past the troubleshooting phase. However, you still need to use certain tools in order to succeed in that task. Once you have identified the problem, you will need to get another set of tools in order to fix it.

This book will focus on the "hardware" tools. These are:

- Screwdrivers – When checking a computer technician's toolkit, you will surely find screwdrivers. Almost all of the big computer parts you'll see today are mounted using screws. If you need to remove these parts, you need to have the right type of screwdriver. This kind of tool is divided into three types:

  o Flat-Blade – Many people refer to this as the *common* or *standard* screwdriver. The screw used with this screwdriver is rarely used today (mainly because the screw's head can be destroyed easily).

  o Phillips – This is perhaps the most popular type of screwdrivers being used today. The screws used with a Phillips screwdriver have enough head surface: you can turn them many times without damaging the screws' head. According to recent reports, more than 90% of the screws used in computers belong to the Phillips-head type.

  o Torx – This is the type of screwdriver you use while working on tiny screws found on Apple and Compaq computers. The screws you remove using a Torx screwdriver have the most surface to work against: they offer the best resistance in terms of screw-head damage. Nowadays, Torx-type screws are gaining more popularity because of their clean and technical look.

- Flashlight – This is one of the tools you should always have. You'll realize how important this tool is when you're crawling under a table searching for a dropped computer part.

- Needle-Nose Pliers – You should have this in your toolkit. This kind of pliers is great for holding connectors or tiny screws (particularly if you have large hands). If needle-nose pliers are still too big to do certain tasks, you may use a pair of tweezers.

- Compressed Air – While working on a computer, you will usually remove the machine's case first. Once the cover is removed, it would be great if you will clean the computer's internal components. The clumps of dirt and fibers can block airflow inside the system unit. As a result, the PC's life will be shortened. The ideal way to eliminate the dust is by using compressed air.

  If you are working for a big company, you probably have a core air compressor that supplies compressed air. If this kind of compressor is not available, you may purchase canned compressed air. However, you'll be shelling out large amounts of money – cans of compressed air are expensive.

- Soldering Iron – You can use it to splice broken wires. Nowadays, computer technicians rarely use this tool. Here's the reason: modern computer parts are created with quick-disconnect connectors. You can easily replace them without splicing anything.

- Wire Strippers – Whenever you have to solder something, you need to use a stripper/wire cutter to prepare the wires for connection. Stripping means you will expose a certain part of the wire by removing the insulation.

- Multi-Meters – This tool is named as such because it is basically a set of different types of testing meters, such as ammeter, voltmeter, and ohmmeter. When used by a trained technician, a multi-meter can identify the failure of various types of computer parts.

  A multi-meter has an analog or digital display, a mode selector switch, and two probes. You can use the switch to perform two things: (1) select the function you want to test and (2) choose the range in which the meter will work. If you need to use an old meter to measure a power pack, you should manually set the range selector. Modern multi-meters, particularly the digital ones, can automatically find the correct ranges.

  Important Note: You should never measure voltage by connecting a manual ranging multi-meter to an AC electrical outlet. This will damage the meter itself, the meter mechanisms, or both.

How to Measure Resistance Using a Multi-Meter

Resistance is the property of electricity commonly measured when troubleshooting computer parts. This electrical property is measured in ohms and represented by the Greek letter "omega." If a multi-meter indicates infinite resistance, the electric currents cannot travel from one prove to another. If you are using a multi-meter to check the resistance and you are getting an infinite reading, there's a huge possibility that the wire is broken.

When measuring resistance, you should set the tool to measure ohms. You can do it using either the selector dial or the front button. Then, connect the PC component you want to measure between the tool's probes. The multi-meter will then show the component's resistance value.

How to Measure Voltage Using a Multi-Meter

This process is similar to the one discussed above, but with two main differences:

1. While measuring voltage, make sure that you properly connect each probe to the source of electricity. For DC voltage, the "-" should be connected to the negative side and the "+" to the positive one. This positioning is irrelevant when measuring AC voltage.

2. You should switch the selector to Volts DC (VDC) or Volts AC (VAC), depending on what you need to measure, to instruct the tool about the voltage you are working with. These settings protect the tool from overload. The multi-meter will blow up if you will plug it into a power source while it's still on "measure resistance" mode.

Chapter 5: Operating Systems

The CompTIA A+ examination will test your knowledge regarding operating systems. Since operating systems play an important role in the computer industry, you should be familiar with them. This chapter will guide you in this topic. Here, you'll learn different things about a computer's OS.

What is an Operating System?

Computers are useless if they don't have any piece of software. Well, you can use them as a doorstop or paperweight – but that is not cost-efficient. You need to have an interface before you can use the capabilities of a computer. And, if you don't know yet, software acts as the interface. Although there are different kinds of software, or computer programs, the most important one you'll ever need is the OS.

Operating systems have various functions, most of which are extremely complex. However, two functions are critical:

1. Interfacing with the computer's hardware

2. Providing an environment in which other pieces of software can run.

Here are the three main types of software that you will encounter in the CompTIA exam:

- Operating System – It provides a stable environment for other computer programs. In addition, it allows the user to enter and execute commands. The operating system gives the user an interface so they can enter commands (i.e. input) and get results or feedback (i.e. output). For this, the OS should communicate with the PC's hardware and conduct the tasks below:

  o Device access

  o Output format

  o Memory management

  o File and disk management

  Once the operating system has performed these basic tasks, the user can enter instructions to the computer using an input device (e.g. a mouse or keyboard). Some of the commands are pre-installed in the operating system, whereas others are given using certain applications. The OS serves as the platform on which the PC's hardware, other pieces of software, and the user work together.

- Application – This is used to complete a specific task. Basically, an application is a computer program written to support the commands given to the OS. Every application is compiled or configured for the operating system it will be used for. Because of this, the application depends on the OS to perform most of its basic functions.

  When a program accesses the computer's memory and linked devices, it sends a request to the OS. The machine's operating system will perform the requests made by the program being used. This setup helps greatly in decreasing the programming overhead, since most of the executable codes are shared – they are written onto the operating system and can be used by different applications installed on the computer.

- Driver – This is an extremely specific program created to instruct an operating system on how to access and use a piece of hardware (e.g. webcam, flash memory, etc.). Every webcam or flash memory has distinct features and settings – the driver helps the OS in knowing how the new hardware works and the things it can do.

The Terms and Concepts Related to Operating Systems

In this section, let's define some of the most important terms and concepts. Study this section carefully since it will teach you the terms you'll encounter during the CompTIA A+ exam.

Key Terms

- Source – This is the code that explains how computer programs work. An operating system can be open source or closed source.

  - Open Source – The users have the right to change and examine the code.

  - Closed Source – The users are not allowed to edit or check the code.

- Version – This is a specific variant of a computer program, usually expressed by a number, which informs users regarding the "newness" of the software. For instance, MS-DOS is now in its sixth main version. Computer programmers distinguish minor revisions from major ones this way:

  - "Program" 4.0 to "Program" 5.0 is a major revision.

  - "Program" 5.0 to "Program" 5.2 is a minor revision.

- Shell – A piece of software that works on top of the operating system. It allows users to execute commands through an array of menus or a different type of graphical interface. A shell makes an operating system simpler and easier to use by modifying the GUI (graphical user interface).

- GUI – The method by which a user communicates with computers. A GUI uses a touchpad, mouse, or a different mechanism (aside from a keyboard) to interact with the machine and issue commands.

- Multithreading – The capability of a computer program to contain several requests in the computer's CPU. Since it allows an application to perform different tasks simultaneously, computers experience a boost in performance and efficiency.

- Network – A group of computers that are connected by a communication link. A network allows computers to share resources and information.

- Preemptive Multitasking – This is a multitasking technique in which the operating system allocates each program a certain amount of CPU time. Afterward, the OS takes back the control and provides another task or program access to the CPU. Basically, if a computer program crashes, the operating system takes the processor from the faulty program and gives it to the next one (which must be working). Even though unstable computer programs still get locked, only the affected application will stop – not the whole machine.

- Cooperative Multitasking – This is a multitasking technique that relies on the applications themselves. Here, each program is responsible for utilizing and giving up access to the CPU. Windows 3.1 used this method to manage multiple programs. If an application stalls while it is using the CPU, the application fails to free the CPU properly, and the whole computer gets locked, the user needs to reboot the machine.

Conclusion

Thank you again for purchasing this book!

I hope this book was able to help you to prepare for the CompTIA A+ tests.

The next step is to reread this book and use other information sources. That way, you can increase your chances of passing the exam.

Finally, if you enjoyed this book, please take the time to share your thoughts and post a review on Amazon. It'd be greatly appreciated!

Thank you and good luck!

Book 2

Human-Computer Interaction

By Solis Tech

The Fundamentals Made Easy!

Human-Computer Interaction: The Fundamentals Made Easy!

Table of Contents

Human-Computer Interaction: The Fundamentals Made Easy!

Introduction

I want to thank you and congratulate you for purchasing the book, "**Human-Computer Interaction: The Fundamentals Made Easy!**"

This book contains proven steps and strategies on how to conceptualize and design a computer system that incorporate principles on effective interaction between the user and the device.

Human-computer interaction (HCI) is the study of the interaction between people and computers and the degree at which computers are developed enough to successfully interact with humans. So many institutions particularly academic and corporations now study HCI. Unfortunately, ease-of-use has not been a priority to most computer systems developer. The issue continues to bedevil the HCI community as accusations still abound that computer makers are still indifferent and are not making enough effort to make truly user-friendly products.

On the other hand, the designing task of computer system developers is not simple either as computers are very complex products. It is also true that the demand for use of computers have grown by leaps and bounds outstripping the need for ease-of-use by a significant margin. If you are a computer designer or simply have basic interest in making devices more effective for users, this book will help you a lot.

Thanks again for purchasing this book, I hope you enjoy it!

Chapter 1: Aspects of HCI

Main aspects of HCI

HCI is composed of three main features, namely: the user, the computer, and their interaction or how they work together.

"User" refers to either the individual or the group of users doing things together. An understanding of how the people's sense of sight, hearing, and touch send information is very important. Also, the type of mental models of interactions differs according to the personality of the user. And finally, interactions are also influenced by cultural and national differences.

"Computer," on the other hand, pertains to all technology from desktop to huge computer systems. As an example, if the topic is website design, the computer would then be the website. "Computers" would also include gadgets like mobile phones or even VCRs.

Finally, the "Interaction" is what happens as "User" uses the "Computer" to achieve a certain objective. Humans, of course, are totally different from machines. So the HCI's main intent is to ensure a successful interaction between the two.

In this aspect, adequate knowledge about humans and computers are critical to realize a functioning system. You need to seek inputs from users. Such knowledge would provide much needed information in determining schedule and budget that are crucial to the systems. In effect there are ideal situations and perfect systems. But the key is finding the balance between what is ideal and what is really feasible given the existing situation.

Objectives of HCI

HCI aims to come up with systems that are functional, usable, and safe. Developing computer systems with excellent usability depends on:

- having enough understanding of the aspects that lead people to use technology in certain ways
- being able to devise tools and ways for creating suitable systems
- the development of safe, effective, and efficient interaction

- making people the priority

The main philosophy underneath HCI is that the users or the people using the computers always come first. Developers must always be guided by the users' needs and preferences in designing systems. It is the system that should match the requirements of human users and not people changing to suit the nature of the machines.

The primacy of usability

Usability is one of the principal considerations in HCI. It is simply about ensuring that a system can be easily learned and used or be what is called user-friendly. A system is considered usable if it:

- can be learned easily
- can be remembered easily in terms of use
- is effective
- is efficient
- is safe
- is enjoyable

Lack of usability means wasted time, mistakes, and disappointments. Unfortunately, a lot of existing systems and devices have been designed without sufficient attention to usability. These include ATM, the Web, computer, printer, mobile phone, personal organizer, coffee machine, remote control, soft drink machine, ticket machine, photocopier, stereo, watch, video game, library information systems, and calculator.

A good example is the photocopier. If you are not familiar with the symbols on the buttons you will be greatly confused. For instance, the big button with the C on it actually refers to Clear, not Copy. The button used to produce copies is actually on the left side with an unrelated symbol. Devices and gadgets should be easy, effortless, and enjoyable to use.

Analyzing and designing a system based on HCI principles involve a lot of factors that produce really complex analysis because of interactions among many of them. The major factors are:

- The User – motivation, satisfaction, experience, enjoyment, personality. Also cognitive processes and capabilities

- User Interface – navigation, output devices, icons, commands, input devices, graphics, dialogue structures, user support, use of color, multimedia, natural language
- Environmental Factors – health and safety, noise, heating, lighting, ventilation
- Organization Factors – job design, work organization, training, roles, politics
- Task Factors – task allocation, skills, easy, novel, complex, monitoring
- Comfort Factors – seating, layout, equipment
- Constraints – budgets, buildings, cost, equipment, timescales, staff
- Productivity Factors – decrease costs, increase quality, increase innovation, increase output, decrease errors
- System Functionality – software, hardware, application

There are different disciplines representing a wide array of subjects that are covered in HCI. The manifold inputs from these fields have continued to enrich HCI. The disciplines include:

- Cognitive Psychology – limitations, performance predictions, information processing, cooperative working, capabilities
- Ergonomics – display readability, hardware design
- Computer Science – graphics, software design, prototyping tools, technology, User Interface Management Systems (UIMS) and User Interface Development Environments (UIDE)
- Social Psychology – social and organizational structures
- Engineering and Design – engineering principles, graphic designs
- Linguistics – natural language interfaces
- Philosophy, Sociology, and Anthropology – computer supported cooperative work (CSCW)
- Artificial Intelligence – intelligent software

Chapter 2: The Human Side in the HCI

Some of the key aspects that shed light on the human side of HCI are:

1. <u>Perceptual-Motor Interaction</u>. Effective human-computer interface design requires an appreciation of the whole human perceptual-motor system. The information-processing approach is central to the perceptual-motor behavior study and for considering the human factors in HCI. An effective interface design reflects the designer's knowledge of the perceptual such as visual displays, use of sound, and graphics. Also the cognitive exemplified by conceptual models and desktop metaphors as well as motoric constraints like ergonomic keyboards of the human perpetual-motor system.

   Man has gone beyond the use of computer punch cards and command-line interfaces. We now use speech recognition, eye-gaze control, and graphical user interfaces. The importance of various perceptual, cognitive, and motor constraints of the human system is now better recognized in HCI. An effective interface must take into account the perceptual and action expectations of users, the action that is seen with a response location, and the mapping of the perceptual-motor workspaces.

2. <u>Human Information Processing.</u> Aspects of human information processing such as models, theories, and methods are currently well developed. The available knowhow in this field is broadly useful to HCI in general such as in the representation and communication of knowledge and visual display design. An effective HCI requires making the interaction compatible with the human information-processing capabilities. Many things about human information processing have been integrated into cognitive architectures that are now applicable to HCI. These applications include the Model Human Processor, the Act model, the SOAR model, and the Epic model.

3. <u>Mental Models in Human–Computer Interaction.</u> Studying mental models can help understand HCI by inspecting the processes by which such models impact behavior. For example, mental models of machines can enable both novice and seasoned problem solvers to find new methods for fulfilling a task through more elaborate encoding of remembered methods.

   The Reverse Polish Notation is a great example of this. There is also a general theory that says readers develop a representation in their mind at several levels of what they read. First is the encoding of text, followed by the representation of propositional content of text. Finally, to this text, they integrate world knowledge to form a mental model of the situation described.

Readers also have the ability to look for ideas in multiple texts. They construct a kind of structured mental maps that show which documents contained which ideas even when they did not expect to need it while reading. Mental models are generally considered as semantic knowledge. Focusing on the degree of commonality among team members, for instance, when it comes to knowledge and beliefs, allows quantitative measures of similarity and differences which is the language of computers.

4. Emotion in Human–Computer Interaction. Emotion used to be persona non grata in the field of computer design. It had no place in the efficiency and rationality of computers which were the personification of zero emotion. Recent study findings in the field of psychology and technology show in a totally different light the relationship between humans, computers, and emotions.

Emotion has ceased to be considered only in light of anger generated by inexplicable computer crashes or hyper excitement caused by video games. Nowadays, it is widely accepted that a host of emotions are important part of computer-related activities such as Web search, sending an email, online shopping, and playing computer games. In almost everything now, the emotional systems get engaged according to psychologists.

Studies and discussions on emotion and computers have grown a lot because of dramatic advances in technology. Computers have actually been used to evaluate the relationship between emotion and its correlates. In the same vein, the astounding improvements in quality and speed of signal processing now enable computers to form conclusion on a user's emotional condition. Compared to purely textual interfaces that have very limited range, the multimodal interfaces that can use voices, faces, and bodies are now more capable to a broader range of emotions.

Nowadays, the performance of an interface will be seriously impeded without considering the user's emotional state. Surprisingly, it can earn even descriptions like socially inept, incompetent, and cold. Much remains to be done to successfully incorporate emotion recognition into interfaces. Still, more studies about the interaction between design and testing can help create interfaces that are efficient and effective while providing satisfaction and enjoyment.

5. Cognitive Architecture. A cognitive architecture is a computer simulation program that makes use of human cognition principle based on human experimental data. It also refers to software artifacts developed by computer programmers. Likewise, the term also includes large software systems which are considered hard to develop and maintain.

Right now, cognitive architectures are not widely utilized by HCI practitioners. Nevertheless, it is quite relevant as an engineering field to usability and has important applications in computing systems especially in HCI. It also serves as theoretical science in human computer interaction studies. Finally, cognitive architectures combine artificial intelligence methods and knowledge with data and principles from cognitive psychology.

Presently-known cognitive architectures are undergoing improvements and are being utilized in HCI-related tasks. Two of the most well-known systems, EPIC and ACT, are production systems or built around one. All systems have production rules which differ from architecture to architecture. The difference lies on focus and history although there's a certain similarity in intellectual history. They may have more congruence than differences at some levels either because of mutual borrowings or due to the convergence of the science. The third system, Soar, is a bit different than the first two production system models.

The three production systems, Soar, Epic, and ACT-R were developed to present different types of human cognition but showed more similarities than divergence as they developed. It is not easy to describe a value possessed by architecture as advantage because to others it constitutes a disadvantage. For instance, Soar's learning mechanism is very important for modeling the improvement of users for a period of time. But there are many applications also where Soar's features result to harmful side effects that can cause more difficulty in model construction.

6. Task Loading and Stress in HCI. Stress in the form of task loading is central to HCI. The traditional perspective on stress sees it in light of exposure to some adverse environmental situations such as noise and the focus of attention centers on most affected physiological system. A new way of looking at it, however, stems from the findings that all stress effects are mediated through the brain.

And since the brain is mainly focused on ongoing behavior or current task, stress ceases to be a peripheral issue but that the ongoing task becomes the primary source of stress. And this renders stress concerns that are central to all HCI issues. This means computer-based systems which aim at helping people lessen cognitive workload and task complexity actually impose more burdens and stress on them.

The person's coping mechanism for such stress affects their work performance and personal wellbeing. The environment may vary but some mechanisms for appraising stress in all task demands are the same. So for HCI, certain principles and designs for stress are applicable across multiple domains.

There are several theories of stress and performance and their connection to human-computer interaction. Workload and stress are at times considered as varying perspectives on the same problem. There are some general practices for stress mitigation. But quite important for this topic is setting up effective measures of information processing and mental resources. It also includes expounding on task dimensions that are relevant and their relationship to self-regulatory mechanisms.

It is critical to establish how an individual's appraisal of his/her environment can be influenced by personal traits and states. This is because stress can only be understood vis-a-vis interaction between a person and the environment. Lastly, it is better to treat stress at multiple levels whether physiological or organizational when making practical application. Instead of one-dimensional which is bound to fail, multidimensional is better as it considers the person, task, and the physical, social and organizational environments.

The implication is that HCI researchers and practitioners should go beyond the design of interface displays and controls and focus also on the person aspects. What are the things in the individual that affect performance and the physical-social environment where the human-technology interaction happens? It means that the technical principles at work in that situation are not adequate. They cannot develop a complete description of the relationship between resources and cognitive activities.

7. Motivating, Influencing, and Persuading Users. From its former role as tool for scientists, the spread of computer use to all sectors of society has brought new uses for computers. Among those uses are persuading people to change their attitudes and behavior. Nowadays, it is widely accepted that skills in motivating and persuading people are necessary for developing a successful HCI.

Interaction designers are actually agents of influence which unfortunately they have not yet understood and applied. Yet their works often involve creating something that tries to change people though they may not be conscious of it. Among these works are motivating people to register the software, learn an online application, or have product loyalty. Changing people's attitudes is now a common feature in the success of interactive products.

Depending on the types of product, the persuasion factor can either be small or large. At any rate, anything that needs to be marketed needs to be persuasive. The growing use of computing products and the limitless scalability of software makes interaction designers one of the best potential change agents in the future.

Take for example the Web-interaction designers who increasingly are facing more challenge in designing something that will hold the attention and motivation of information seekers. After that, they need to persuade web users to adopt certain behaviors like:

- using a software
- joining a survey
- clicking on the ads
- returning often after bookmarking a site
- buying things online
- releasing personal information
- forming an online community

Being able to persuade people is a measure of success here. But with success comes responsibility. The Web designer needs to make the website credible. The following are some broad guidelines to ensure credibility:

1. Design websites to present the real and practical aspects of the organization.
2. Invest sufficiently in visual design
3. Make websites that people can easily use.
4. Include markers of good quality
5. Use markers of reliability.
6. Avoid too much commercialism on a website
7. Adopt and adjust to the user experience
8. Avoid being amateurish

To sum it all, computer systems have become an inescapable part of everyday life. The interactive experience involving all systems be it mobile phone or desktop can be designed in such a way as to influence the way we think and act. By combining the computing capability with persuasion psychology, computer systems can motivate and persuade. Humans are undoubtedly still superior when it comes to influencing people. But in many areas of endeavor, computer can do what humans cannot even imagine being capable of.

Computers don't sleep and can be designed to keep trying on and on. At the very least, computers provide a new way for modifying how people act and think. Like it or not, the community of HCI professionals is at the forefront of the campaign to make more sensitive and responsive tech products. It can rise to the challenge of helping churn out products that enhance the people's over-all quality of life. Or it can continue being a tool to produce mindless products whose main reason for being into is to make profit for the owners.

8. <u>Human-Error Identification in Human–Computer Interaction</u>. The leap from focusing on human error in technological problems to a less obvious culprit started in the 1940's. It was established during that year that plane pilot error was often designer error. It began to show that design is the key to

substantially reduce human error and this paradigm continued to gather steam particularly in HCI.

It is now common wisdom that human error can be as often as the product of a defective design or as a person making a mistake. The inadequate design fosters activities that lead to errors. A groundbreaking outcome of this new philosophy is that errors are now viewed as totally predictable events instead of seeing it as unpredictable occurrences. This makes errors avoidable.

So errors became instances where planned series of steps and activities fail to realize intended results independent of any outside change agencies. If errors are no longer random, then it can be identified and predicted ahead of time. What partially drove this line of thinking are the accidents that happened in the nuclear industry that is hungry for preemptive solutions. This has led to the formulation of several human-error identification (HEI) techniques.

Although evaluative and summative in nature, these HEI techniques that employ ergonomics methods can now be used in formative design stages especially in analytic prototyping. For instance, the entry of computer-aided design such as in architecture has profound impacts on prototyping. It made possible what was considered as impossible or too prohibitively costly design alteration at the structural prototyping stage.

The three main forms of prototyping human interfaces have been identified namely: functional analysis, scenario analysis, and structural analysis.

Functional analysis includes consideration of the functional range supported by the device. In comparison, scenario analysis is exemplified by consideration of the device in relation to events sequence. An example of the structural analysis, on the other hand, is the use of user-centered viewpoint in a non-destructive testing of the interface.

One compelling example of the crucial role of design in predicting and minimizing errors concern human error identification (HEI) tools like the TAFEI or Task Analysis for Error Identification. The results of the application of TAFEI on interface project designs show how it can improve systems and its relevance to other ergonomic methods. It served to validate what has been long suspected when it comes to error-design relationship as follow:

- Structured systems like TAFEI results to reliable and trustworthy error data;

- Most errors resulting from technology are totally predictable;

- To improve design and reduce errors, ergonomics methods should be employed in formative design process.

Exploring design weaknesses through tools like TAFEI will go a long way in developing and producing devices and gadgets that are tolerant to error.

Chapter 3: The Computer Side in the HCI

The salient points when it comes to the computer side in HCI include:

1. Input Technologies and Techniques. Input devices which are also a classification of computer can detect physical aspects of places, things, and, of course, people. However, its function is never complete without considering the visual feedback corresponding to the input. It is like using a writing instrument without something to write on. Input and output should always go together.

    And in devices with small screens, this is only possible with the help of integrated sensors. If the user or human characteristics are important in a maximized HCI environment, so are input technologies with enough sophistication to meet user-machine interaction requirements. Users can only achieve the task objectives by combining the right feedback with inputs. In this regard, the HCI designer should take into account the following:

a. the industrial and ergonomic design of the gadget

b. the physical censor

c. the relationship among all interaction techniques

Input gadgets have many properties that apply to the usual pointing devices or mobile items with touch input. These pointing devices include the: mice, trackballs, isometric joysticks, isotonic joysticks, indirect tablets, touchpads, touchscreens, and pen-operated devices. The mice or mouse, of course, is one of the most popular as anyone who has ever used a computer knows. Because of its inherent advantages for individual users where it can easily be used by most people, it is one of the most preferred pointing devices.

Touchpads are most well-known to laptop users. These are small tablets that are sensitive to touch and which are usually featured on laptop units. Touchscreens on the other hand are tablets that are sensitive to touch which are placed on a display. It is increasingly becoming the tool to beat because of the proliferation of smart phones and other hand-held devices.

There are input models and theories that are quite helpful in evaluating the efficacy of interaction strategies. But it would be most beneficial to readers here to focus on current and future trends for this feature. Interactive system designers should go beyond the usual things like graphical user interface and pointing ideas when it comes to inputs.

They must delve deeper into more effective search strategies, sensor inputs for new data types, and techniques of synthesis to make much better sense of data. Better search tools will enhance navigation and manual search regarding file systems. One outstanding development is the breakthrough in the development of more advanced sensor inputs such as technologies for tagging and location.

It allows computers to identify physical objects and locations that have been tagged, and to detect their location and distance to other devices through signal strength analysis. These sensors are making interface personalization much easier. This development in interaction also has great implications for data mining and techniques for machine learning. Continuous improvement in structure synthesis and extraction techniques is invaluable in this data-rich era.

An overriding aim in HCI is to achieve dramatic advancement in humanity's interaction with technology. The computer side of this presents limitless possibilities but the cognitive skills and senses of man will be relatively stagnant. Our holding, touching, and object-movement are not the result of technology-like progress but a product of our human limitations.

2. Recognition- and Sensor-Based Input for Interaction. Computers are able to manipulate physical signals that have been transformed by sensors into electrical signals. Sensors have found their way into various fields of industry such as robotics, automotive, and aerospace. It has also found vast applications in consumer products.

    The computer mouse is a very good example. Imagine that simple-looking device equipped with algorithms that process images and specialized camera that enables it to be unbelievably sensitive to motions. It detects movement at the rate of a thousand of an inch several thousand times per second. Another interesting device is the accelerometer that detects acceleration due to movement and continuous acceleration because of gravity.

    Digital cameras now make use of accelerometers to save a photo. Laptops also are equipped with accelerometers for self-protection. When the laptop is accidentally dropped the accelerometer enables the hard disk to secure the hard drive prior to impact. With smartphones, the goal is for motion sensing for the purpose of interaction such as determining the walking pattern of users. Generally, HCI research on sensors dwells on its usage to improve interaction.

    Sensor studies are either to broaden input options or build new computing forms. The new forms include mobile devices that recognize locations and places that are sensitive to the presence and needs of its inhabitants. Still there are far more advanced goals and applications like in robotics.

41

There is a race to develop machines that will behave and think like humans or at least complement their capabilities. It has many critical applications such as in nuclear power accident mitigation. One worry, of course, is that it will end up in the military. But in safety, mobile computing, entertainment, productivity, affective computing, and surveillance, sensors are finding widespread application.

An intriguing side note here is the idea of developing a sensor to enable computers to detect and accordingly react to the frustration of its user. The computer's response could be something like playing relaxing music. Sensing could be in the form of the user banging on the keyboard in frustration. A microphone could react to the yelling of the speaker or the webcam could sense scowling.

In general, the potential of interactive sensing is quite good. The degree of progress across the whole computing spectrum actually gives the impression that sky is the limit. Advances in nanotechnology, CPU power, and storage capacities will continue to produce more outstanding innovations in the computer side of HCI.

But what is driving the unprecedented growth of the sensor-based interactive systems is the dizzying expansion in devices outside the old desktop computer. It is hard to keep track of the explosive proliferation of smart phones, tablet PCs, portable gaming devices, music and movie players, living room-centric computers, and personal digital assistants. Computing is becoming part and parcel of our daily life and our environment.

Through recognition techniques and sensing systems, task-specific computing devices will be developed instead of general functions. It will also pave the way for different types of interaction style in HCI. This activity-specific interactive systems development will further hasten innovations on a much broader array of practical applications.

3. Visual Displays. Timekeeping has always been one function that man has strived for a good visual display. Today's smartwatches which are actually wrist computers sport stunning visual displays. It is no longer limited to displaying time but is multifunctional. Some brands can pinpoint exact location in the planet through a global positioning system. Others can show heart rate while a number can be personal digital assistants.

The main idea behind wearable computing is that the human body is wearing the visual displays. One major way people use wearables is to put the display on one's head making user's hands free to work. It is called headmounted displays or HMDs. The screen-based is one category of HMDs. It makes use of the retinal-projection method which projects images on the retina of the eye.

An alternative method is the scanning displays which scan images onto the retina pixel by pixel. A second type of display which is actually much bigger in scope and the most widespread is the hand-held and wrist-worn displays. They are in mobile phones, media players, wristwatches, and other portable gadgets. Apple is one of the global leaders in this field and the most well-known. Even textiles for clothing are now being used for such technology in what is now known as photonic textiles-fabric.

Multicolored lighting systems were merged with the fabrics for its electronic information function without affecting the cloth's softness. It has sensors, GSM, and Bluetooth! Photonic fabrics have great promising applications in the areas of personal health care and communication.

4. <u>Haptic Interfaces</u>. Haptic interface refers to a device for sending feedback that produces sensation of weight, touch, rigidity, and other aspects through the skin and muscle. This force feedback mechanism is designed to enhance computer-human interaction. Because haptics are done through actual physical contact, they are not easy to synthesize unlike the sense of sight and sound that are gathered through the eyes and ears.

   The genius in the haptic interface is that it simply makes use of the body's own highly sophisticated receptor system. The haptic feedback is made possible through synthetic stimulation in the skin and proprioception.

   Proprioception involves something deeper than the skin – the muscle and skeleton. The mechanoreceptors in the body enable its detection of contact forces received from the environment. Body receptors sense velocity, skin stretching, vibration, and edges of objects. Haptic interfaces are more widely applied in the field of virtual reality than in information media and related devices are now available commercially.

Two of the most important research needs on haptic interfaces in the future concern the psychology in haptics and safety considerations. Safety is a crucial issue as insufficient actuator control can lead to injuries for users. Control problems may occur with the tool displays and exoskeleton. Unintended forces or vibration may pose danger to the user.

A locomotion interface that holds a user's body can cause serious physical damage if control is inadequate. It requires proven safety equipment that amply protects the walker and this should be a major objective of research. A much safer alternative is a system where the user does not wear any equipment during the interaction.

The psychology in haptics on the other hand requires more studies on muscle sensation as most existing findings are on skin sensation. Among the few promising findings relate to Laderman and Klatzky's work (1987) on force display and their recent study of forces distributed according to space. Their psychological findings have very promising applications in the development of haptic interface. A lot of obstacles need to be overcome before usage of haptic interface becomes widespread.

Though men cannot do without haptics in real life interaction, it is still of limited use in HCI. One can say haptic interface is still in infancy with its 10-year background. So eventually its time will come just like image displays (e.g. TV and movies) which started 100 years ago. For now, what are available are a few haptic interfaces with limited functionality and high cost. At the very least, haptic interface is a new very promising frontier in HCI with immense potential contribution to man's quality of life.

5. Non-speech Auditory Output. Sound is one of the key aspects that complete our interaction with our environment. But where speech is direct and necessitates focus and attention, non-speech sound is more diffused and provides a different class of information.

   Non-speech sounds include sounds from the environment, music, and sound effects. Nevertheless, speech and non-speech sounds complement each other just like text is complemented by visual symbols. Non-speech sounds can give information in a shorter period of time than speech.

   Right now, the non-speech field needs more research. The user interface is a much more effective tool for HCI when it employs a combined visual and sound feedback. This sound-visual combination has complementary function as well. Visual gives specific information about a small area reached by our eyes but sound or the auditory system provides more general information from beyond our focus.

   Our senses are the key to our effective interaction with the external world. These senses in turn bring more dimensions in information as they enhance one another. These principles are very useful in a multimodal HCI by adding non-speech sound output to the graphical displays. An example of this application is focusing our eyes on one task like editing a manuscript while monitoring other aspects in the machine through sound.

Reliance on visual sense which is more prevalent at present can be problematic. One problem is there could be visual overload which means the user could miss lots of information. Or simply that the viewer cannot look at everything at the same time at all times. Sound can help eliminate that situation by giving information to the user that the eyes could not see.

This interdependence between visual and audio could make information presentation far more efficient. Non-speech sound is mainly used in games' sound effects, music, and other multimedia usages. It is commonly employed in creating a certain mood for the item like in movies. In HCI, sound is used to provide information particularly those things that a user does not see or notice such as what is going on in their computer systems.

It is useful to use non-speech sound in HCI for many reasons. Seeing and hearing in the human body is first of all interdependent. The eyes can give information that is high-resolution only in a limited area of focus. But sounds can be received from all sides of the user: front, above, below, and behind. This not only provides direct information but also tells the eyes where to look to get more useful data. In fact, at times reaction to sound stimuli is faster than what is seen.

Non-speech sound can therefore help in reducing large display overload which can cause users to miss important data. This is especially true in large graphical interfaces that use multiple monitors. Using sound to present some information would reduce screen space. It would also lessen the volume of information that should be on the screen. This is most relevant to gadgets with small visual displays like smartphones and PDAs.

Non-speech sound would also decrease demands on our visual attention. For instance, a user who is walking would miss much information as he looks at his device's visual display because of competing attention from the traffic or uneven surface where he is walking. In fact, if the information is in sound, he does not have to look at his device at all.

Our sense of sound is also underutilized. Yet as exemplified by classical music, its intricate organization can make, say a symphony, a powerful tool for transmitting complex information. The beauty with sound is that it grabs attention. It is easy to avoid looking at something but hard to ignore sound which makes it very effective in sending important information. Likewise, certain things in the interface look more natural in sound than in sight.

Finally, non-speech sound will allow visually-impaired users to use computers. Newer graphical displays have, in particular, made it even harder for them to operate the device. Research has been extensive in the HCI application of non-speech sound in a wide range of topics.

There are two main areas of growth where the application of non-speech sound has the best potential. One is in the creation of multimodal displays that utilizes all available senses. This means integrating sound with other things like force-feedback and tactile apart from sight. The other area is in wearable and mobile computing gadgets that also use multimodal displays.

As mentioned, the screens of these devices are small and sound will reduce the need for screen space.

6. Network-Based Interaction. Networked interfaces have modified our perception of society and the world at large particularly with the Web and now mobile devices. There are several roles that networks play in HCI. The first is as an Enabler which refers to things that can be done only with network. The second is as Mediator which pertains to problems and issues caused by networks.

Third is as Subject which focuses on managing and understanding networks and fourth as Platform which dwells on interface architectures and algorithms. Network includes both the wire-based and the wireless world. Things are rapidly changing especially in the wireless networks. These changes can be classified in two dimensions, namely:

- **Global vs. Local** – refers to the distance by space between the connected points such as machines in the office to global networks like the Internet.

- **Fixed vs. Flexible** – pertains to the nature of the links between points such as fixed devices and gadget that configures itself. More changes are coming because of spreading wireless links. One example is being able to gain access to internet connections and printers of another office by simply plugging a portable device into the Ethernet.

Traditionally, LANs belong to local-fixed category while Internet is global-fixed. Hand-helds like cell phones are also categorized as global-fixed because phones are fixed and independent of location. The internet makes use of domain names which are fixed like URLs. Some phone technologies like GSM and GPRS are classified as global-fixed because it is possible to send content that is based on location. Also the enlarging data capability is enabling services to handle huge media content.

What set these technologies apart, however, are the connectivity model and the charging which are usually by data use or fixed charge. There are a number of current and new technologies from the local-flexible type. These include the Wi-Fi, infrared, Bluetooth, and ZigBee which permit flexible connections among personal gadgets. With them, a computer device can utilize a mobile-phone modem or a headset with Bluetooth can make connections with a phone, wireless. Unfortunately, these capabilities also enhance unsavory activities like illegal equipment accessing, hacking, and surveillance.

7. Wearable Computers. Computers have become like appendage to many office workers. But it is hard for those using mobile devices to get the information

they need. In a mobile situation, existing interfaces will hamper the user's main task. Users will be forced to prioritize the device instead of the environment. The need is for a wearables design that helps fulfill not obstruct the task.

A framework that can be very useful in creating good designs of computer interfaces which are wearable is CAMP. This framework addresses different factors that may impinge on the effectiveness of the design such as body closeness and how it is used. CAMP stands for:

- Corporal – which means absence of discomfort to users during physical interface with the wearable.
- Attention – interface design should allow user to focus both on the real world and virtual reality.
- Manipulation – there are adequate controls which are easy to manipulate particularly in a mobile environment.
- Perception – Design must enable user to quickly perceive displays even when mobile. So displays should be easy to navigate and simple.

Outside offices and buildings, an attractive option for a user to have access to a computer interface is through wearables. There are challenges however that need to be addressed to fulfill the tasks in terms of contextual awareness, interface, adaptation to tasks, and cognitive model. These include:

- **Modalities of Input/output** – the ease of use and accuracy of modalities developed that try to copy the human brain's input/output capacity are not yet satisfactory. Frustrations bedevil users when there are inaccuracies. Also the computing requirement of these modalities is way beyond what low-weight wearable devices have. Input devices which are simple to use are needed.

- **Models of User interface** – there is a need for extensive experimentation in using applications involving end-users.

- **Capability-applications matching** – evaluation and design of interface should prioritize development of most effective way to access information and avoid creating additional features.

- **Simple methodology in interface evaluation** – current evaluation approaches are too complicated and time-consuming making them unsuitable in interface design. What is needed is an evaluation methodology that addresses frustration and human errors.

- **Context awareness** – for context aware computing to be realized, several questions must be answered. These include application models

47

that integrate the social and cognitive aspects, social and cognitive mapping of inputs from many sensors, anticipating the needs of users, and interacting with the users.

Conclusion

Thank you again for purchasing this book!

I hope this book was able to help you to gain useful knowledge and understanding about human-computer interaction.

The next step is to apply what you have learned.

Finally, if you enjoyed this book, please take the time to share your thoughts and post a review on Amazon. It'd be greatly appreciated!

Thank you and good luck!